**1**

2

# The Plans
## of
# The Lord
# God:
# Jeremiah 29 : 11

## By

## John C Burt

**4**

Photographs Courtesy
of :
eleventh - wave.
lse - library.
francois - genon.
tawan - rapipong.
erwan - hesry.
ludomil.
florian - van-schreven.

Free Downloads on :
unsplash.com

**5**

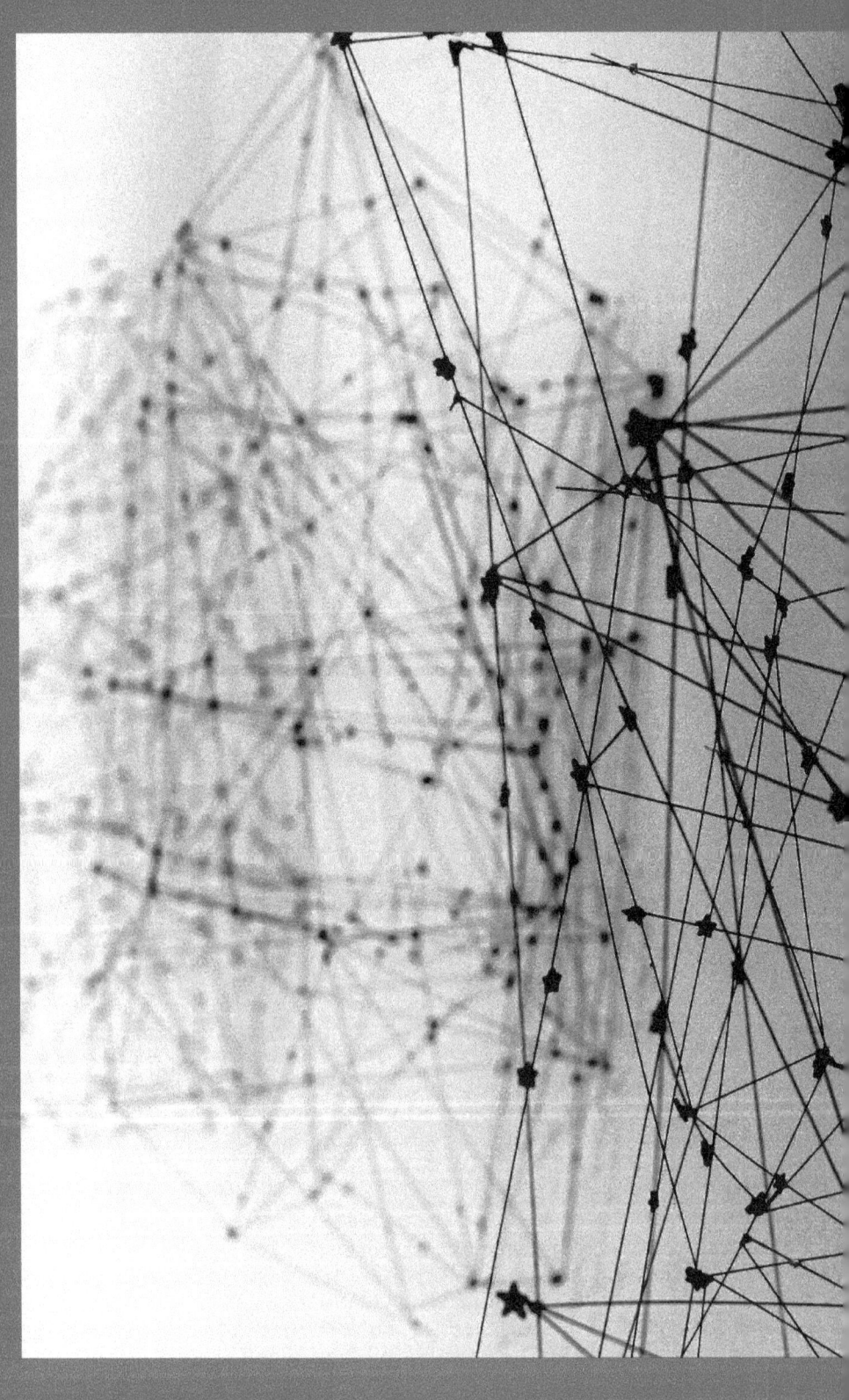

# 1.

## FOREWORD :

As I write this the world - at - large is gripped by Covid - 19 ?

The virus; Covid - 19 is having widespread effects throughout the world - at - large, people getting sick from it and sadly some dying from it. I wanted to do something that ...

23

may in reality, lift the very spirits of the Body of the Lord Jesus Christ Worldwide. You may think that is a big ask and yet, the very Word of God does speak into such a situation as we ...

24

have now in the world - at - large?

    I want to look at things through the lens of Jeremiah 29 : 11. (ESV) " For I know the plans I have for you, declares the LORD,

plans for welfare
and not for evil.
to give you a
future and a
hope. "

In this book,
I want to spend a
lot of time
thinking through
what this is
saying in the ...

midst of the present crisis we all are facing with Covid - 19? I am of the real belief it has much to say to us all in our very days and in our generations. This book will be one that explores some of these ideas, concepts and notions ... Furthermore, we will seek to connect the major themes of Jeremiah 29 : 11 with the rest of the Word of God.

28

Some of
these themes
include such
things as future
and a hope in the
Lord God
Almighty. Today,
we all need to
understand these
two themes more
than ever !

You may well wonder why the pictures of sailing boats dotted throughout this book? It would seem to me , that we are all on a journey in our ...

**30**

own little sailing boats , the journey of life ... In the world - at - large with Covid - 19 this imagery has never been more and more real? We are all on a journey towards the heavenly city,

**31**

the New
Jerusalem ... an
eternity with the
Lord God
Almighty for
those who follow
the Son of God,
the Lord Jesus
Christ ... This
journey can go
through waters ..
32

that are stormy
and yet we are
protected by our
sailing boat and
ultimately the
Lord God
Almighty
Himself ....
          Let the
journey of this
very book begin!

**33**

# 2.

We will look at four different versions of the texts. The

ESV, the NIV, the Voice and finally the GNT. In each case  ..... Jeremiah 29 : 11 will be cited first !

# { ESV }

## Jeremiah 29 : 11

" (11)  For I know the plans I have for you, declares the LORD, plans for welfare and not for evil, to give you a future and a hope . "

**46**

## Proverbs 23 : 18.

" (18) Surely there is a future, and your hope will not be cut off."

## Proverbs 24 : 13 - 14.

" (13) My son, eat honey, for it is good, and the drippings of the honeycomb are sweet to your taste.

47

*(14) Know that wisdom is such to your soul; if you find it, there will be a future, and your hope will not be cut off."*

**Isaiah 40 : 30 - 31.**

**48**

" (30) Even youths shall faint and be weary, and young men shall fall exhausted; (31) but they who wait for the LORD shall renew their strength; they shall mount up with wings like eagles; they shall run and not be weary; they shall walk and not faint. "

49

# Luke 21 : 25 - 28.

"(25)" And there will be signs in sun and moon and stars, and on the earth distress of nations in perplexity because of the roaring of the sea and the waves, (26) people fainting

50

with fear and with foreboding of what is coming on the world. For the powers of the heavens will be shaken."

(27) And then they will see the Son of Man coming in a cloud with power and great glory.

*(28) Now when these things begin to take place, straighten up and raise your heads, because your redemption is drawing near."*

**John 17 : 24.**

52

" (24) Father, I desire that they also, whom you have given me, may be with me where I am, to see my glory that you have given me because you loved me before the foundation of the world."

# Acts 17 : 30 - 31.

" (30) The times of ignorance God overlooked, but now he commands all people everywhere to repent,
(31) because he has fixed a day on which he will judge the world in righteousness by

54

a man who he has appointed; and of this he has given assurance to all by raising him from the dead . "

## Ephesians 1 : 17 - 23.

" (17) that the God of our Lord Jesus Christ, the Father of glory, may give you the Spirit of wisdom and of

55

revelation in the knowledge of him, (18) having the eyes of your hearts enlightened , that you may know what is the hope to which he has called you, what are the riches of his glorious inheritance in the saints, (19) and what is the immeasurable ...

56

greatness of his power
toward us who believe,
according to the
working of his great
might

(20) that he
worked in Christ when
he raised him from the
dead and seated him at
his right hand in the
heavenly places,

(21) far above all rule and authority and power and dominion, and above every name that is named, not only in this age but also in the one to come.

(22) And he put all things under his

feet and gave him as head over all things to the church,

(23) which is his body, the fullness of him who fills all in all."

**Colossians 1 : 3 - 6.**

**59**

" (3) We always thank Go, the Father of our Lord Jesus Christ, when we pray for you, (4) since we heard of your faith in Christ Jesus and of the love that you have for all the saints, (5) because of the hope laid up for you in heaven. Of this you have heard before in the word

**60**

of the truth, the gospel,
(6) which has
come to you, as indeed in
the whole world it is
bearing fruit and
increasing - as it also
does among you, since
the day you heard it and
understood the grace of
God in truth, "

# 1 Timothy 6 : 17 - 19.

" (17) As for the rich in this present age, charge them not to be haughty, nor to set their hopes on the uncertainty of riches, but on God, who richly provides us with everything to enjoy.

62

(18) They are to do good, to be rich in good works, to be generous and ready to share,

(19) thus storing up treasure for themselves as a good foundation for the future, so that they may take hold of that which is truly life."

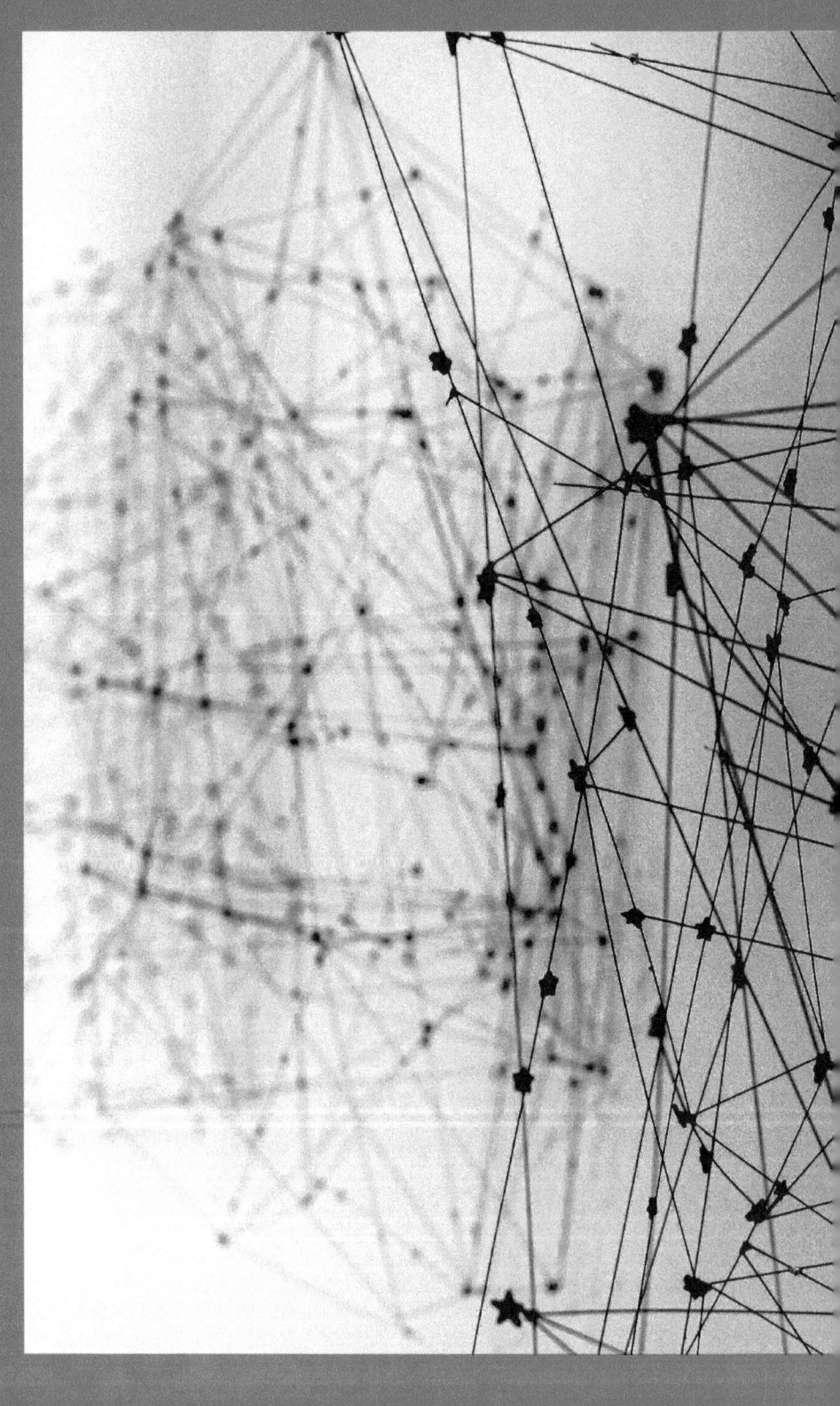

# 3.

## { NIV }

Jeremiah 29 : 11

76

" (11) "For I know the plans I have for you ", declares the LORD, " Plans to prosper you and not to harm you, plans to give you hope and a future." "

**Proverbs 23 : 18**

77

" ( 18 ) There is surely a future hope for you, and your hope will not be cut off."

**Proverbs 24 : 13 - 14.**

" (13) Eat honey, my son, for it is good; honey from the comb is sweet to your taste.

**78**

*(14) Know also that wisdom is like honey for you: If you find it, there is a future hope for you, and your hope will not be cut off."*

**Isaiah 40 : 30 - 31.**

**79**

" (30) Even youths grow tired and weary, and young men stumble and fall;

(31) but hose who hope in the LORD will renew their strength. They will soar on wings like eagles; they will run and not grow weary, they will walk and not be faint."

**80**

" (25) " There will be signs in the sun, moon and stars. On the earth, nations will be in anguish and perplexity at the roaring and tossing of the sea.

(26) People will faint from terror, apprehensive of what is

coming on the world, for the heavenly bodies will be shaken.

(27) At that time they will see the Son of Man coming in a cloud with power and great glory.

(28) When these things begin to take place, stand up and lift up your heads, because

your redemption is
drawing near."

## John 17 : 24.

"(24) " Father, I
want those you have
given me to be with me
where I am, and to see
my glory, the glory you
have given me because
you loved me before the

creation of the world." "

## Acts 17 : 30 - 31.

" (30) In the past God overlooked such ignorance, but now he commands all people everywhere to repent.

(31) For he set a day when he will judge the world with justice by the man he has appointed. He has given proof of this to everyone by raising him from the dead." "

**Ephesians 1 : 17 - 23.**

" (17) I keep
asking that the God of
our Lord Jesus Christ,
the glorious Father, may
give you the Spirit of
wisdom and revelation,
so that you may know
him better.

(18) I pray
that the eyes of your
heart may be enlightened

86

in order that you may know the hope to which he has called you, the riches of his glorious inheritance in his holy people,

(19) and his incomparably great power for us who believe. That power is the same as the mighty strength...

87

(20) he exerted when he raised Christ from the dead and seated him at his right hand in the heavenly realms, (21) far above all rule and authority, power and dominion, and every name that is invoked, not only in the present age but also in the one to come.

**88**

(22) And God placed all things under his feet and appointed him to be head over everything for the church,

(23) which is his body, the fullness of him who fills everything in every way."

**Colossians 1 : 3 - 6.**

" (3) We always thank God, the Father of our Lord Jesus Christ, when we pray for you,

(4) because we have heard of your faith in Christ Jesus and of the love you have for all God's people -

(5) the faith

**90**

and love that spring
from the hope stored up
for you in heaven and
about which you have
already heard in the true
message of the gospel
(6) that has
come to you. In the
same way, the gospel is
bearing fruit and
growing throughout the
whole world - just as it

has been doing among you since the day you heard it and truly understood God's grace ."

## 1 Timothy 6 : 17 - 19.

" (17) Command those who are rich in this present world not to be

arrogant nor to put
their hope in wealth,
which is uncertain, but
to put their hope in God,
who richly provides for
us with everything for
our enjoyment.
(18)
Command them to do
good, to be rich in good
deeds, and to be
generous and willing to

share.

(19) In this way they will lay up treasure for themselves as a firm foundation for the coming age, so that they may take hold of the life that is truly life."

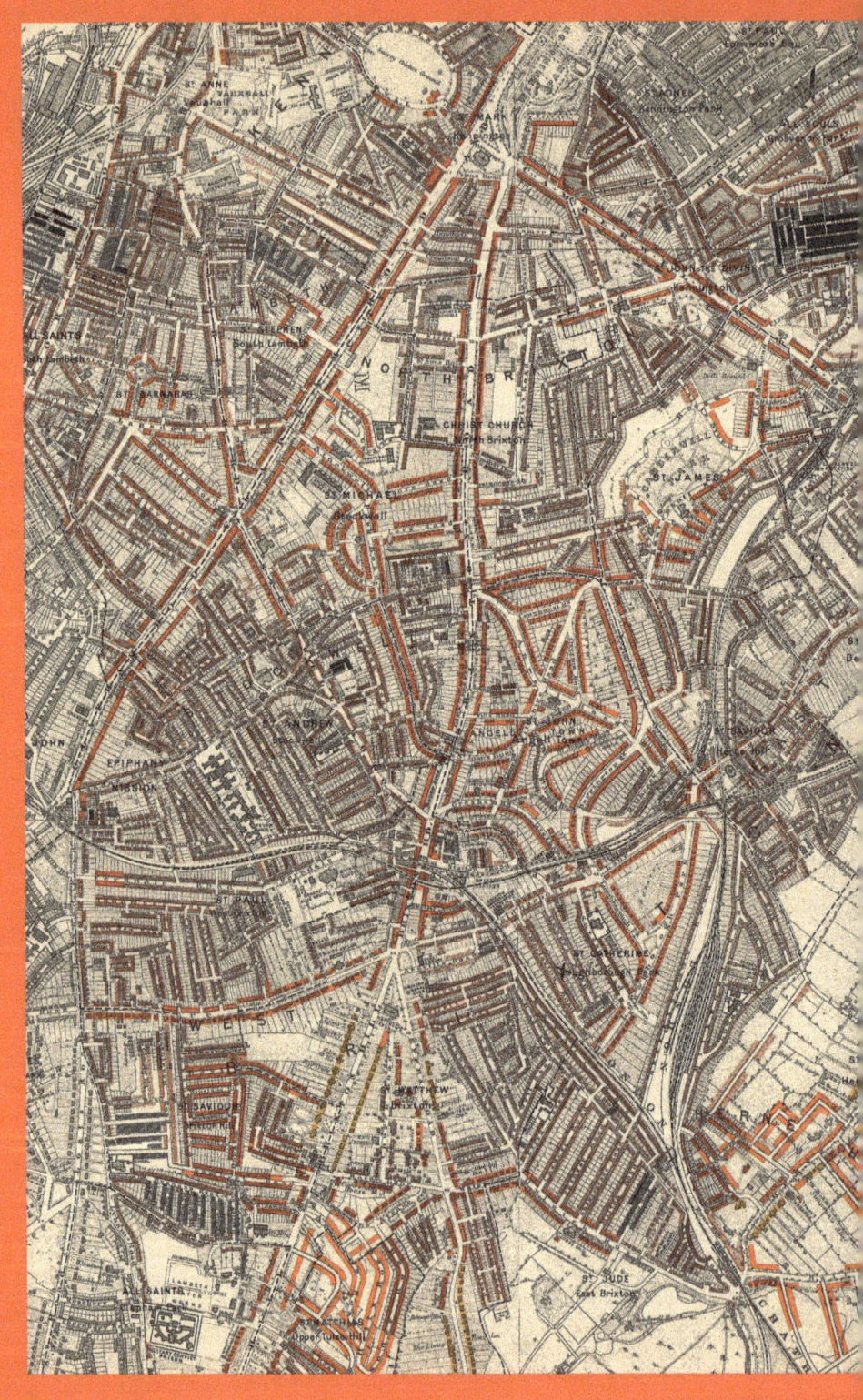

# 4.

# { The Voice}

108

# Jeremiah 29 : 11.

" (11) " For I know the plans I have for you, " says the Eternal, " plans for peace, not evil, to give you a future and hope - never forget that. " "

109

# Proverbs 23 : 18.

*" (18) Your future with Him will be certain, and you will not have hoped in vain. "*

# Proverbs 24 : 13 - 14.

**110**

" (13) My son, eat honey- it's good for you; the honey that drips from the comb is sweet in your mouth.

(14) Know, too, that wisdom is good for your soul; if you find it , your reward will be a bright future and an enduring hope."

**111**

# Isaiah 40 : 30 - 31.

" (30) Young men will get tired; strapping young men will stumble and fall.

(31) But hose who trust in the Eternal One will regain their strength.

They will run -

112

never winded, never
weary.
        They will walk - never
tired , never faint. "

## Luke 21 : 25 - 28.

        " (25) There will
be earth - shattering
events - the heavens
themselves will seem to be
shaken with signs in the
sun, in the moon, and in

the stars. And across the earth the outsider nations will feel powerless and terrified in the face of a roaring flood of fear and foreboding, crashing like tidal waves upon them.

(26) " What's happening to the world?" people will wonder. The cosmic order will be ....

destabilized.

(27) And then, at that point, they will see the Son of Man coming in a cloud with power and blazing glory.

(28) So when the troubles begin, don't be afraid. Look up - raise your head high, because the truth is that your liberation is fast approaching."

**115**

# John 17 : 24.

" (24) Father, I long for the time when those You have given Me can join Me in My place so they may witness My glory, which comes from You. You have loved Me before the foundations of

**116**

the cosmos were laid."

"Paul (30) No, God has patiently tolerated this kind of ignorance in the past, but now God says it is time to rethink our lives and reject these unenlightened assumptions."

(31) He has fixed a day of accountability, when the whole world will be justly evaluated by a new higher standard; not by a statute , but by a living man. God selected this man and made Him credible to all by raising Him from the dead."

**118**

# Ephesians 1 : 17 - 23.

" (17) God of our Lord Jesus the Anointed, Father of Glory: I call out to You on behalf of Your people. Give them minds ready to receive wisdom and revelation so they will ...

truly know You.

(18) Open the eyes of their hearts, and let the light of Your truth flood in. Shine Your light on the hope You are calling them to embrace. Reveal to them the glorious riches You are preparing as their inheritance.

(19) Let them see

the full extent of Your power that is at work in those of us who believe, and may it be done according to Your might and power.

Friends, it is the same might and resurrection power that (20) He used in the Anointed One to raise Him from the dead and to position Him at His right hand in heaven. There is nothing over Him.

(21) He's above all rule, authority, power, and dominion; over every name invoked, over every title bestowed in this age and the next.

(22) God has

placed all things beneath His feet and anointed Him as the head over all things for His church. (23) This church is His body, the fullness of the One who fills all in all. "

Colossians 1 : 3 - 6.

123

" (3) As always, we've been praying for you, thanking God, the Father of our lord Jesus the Anointed, (4) ever since we heard of your faith in Jesus the Anointed and your love for His holy ones -

**124**

(5) a faith and love that emerge from the hope you have heard about in the word of truth - the gospel - the very hope that awaits you in heaven.

(6 - 7) The same gospel that was brought to you is growing and bearing fruit all over the world, just as it has been growing among you

since the day you heard
and took the truth of
God's grace from our
beloved fellow servant
Epaphras  ( He is a
faithful minister of the
Anointed on our
behalf.) "

1 Timothy 6 : 17 -
19.

" (17) Here's what you say to those wealthy in regard to this age: " Don't become high and mighty or place all your hope on a gamble for riches; instead, fix your hope on God, the One who richly provides everything for our enjoyment. "

**127**

(18) Tell them to use their wealth for good things ; be rich in good works! If they are willing to give generously and share everything,

(19) then they will send ahead a great treasure for themselves and build their futures on a solid foundation. As a result, they will surely

*take hold of eternal life."*

129

# 5.

## { GNT }

### Jeremiah 29 : 11.

144

" (11) I alone know the plans I have for you, plans to bring you prosperity and not disaster; plans to bring about the future you hope for. "

**Proverbs 23 : 17 - 18.**

145

" (17) Don't be envious of sinful people; let reverence for the LORD be the concern of your life.

(18) If it is, you have a bright future. "

**Proverbs 24 : 13 - 14.**

146

" (13) My child, eat honey; it is good. And just as honey from the comb is sweet on your tongue,

(14) you may be sure that wisdom is good for the soul. Get wisdom and you have a bright future. "

# Isaiah 40 : 30 - 31.

" (30) Even those who are young grow weak; young people can fall exhausted.

(31) But those who trust in the LORD for help will

*find their strength renewed .*

*They will rise on wings like eagles; they will run and not get weary; they will walk and not grow weak. "*

**Luke 21 : 25 - 28.**

149

" (25) " There will be strange things happening to the sun, the moon, and the stars. On earth whole countries will be in despair, afraid of the roar of the sea and the raging tides.

(26) People will faint from fear as

**150**

they wait for what is coming over the whole earth, for the powers in space will be driven from their courses.

(27) Then the Son of Man will appear, coming in a cloud with great power and glory.

(28) When these things begin to ...

*happen, stand up and raise your heads, because your salvation is near."*

## John 17 : 24.

*" (24) " Father ! You have given them to me, and I want them to be with me where I am,*

152

so that they may see my glory, the glory you gave me; for you loved me before the world was made. "

## Acts 17 : 30 - 31.

" (30) God has overlooked the times when people did not know him, but now he commands all of them everywhere to turn away from their evil ways.

(31) For he has fixed a day in which he will judge the whole world with justice by means of a man he has chosen. He has given proof of this to everyone

by raising that man
from death! "

**Ephesians 1 : 17
- 23.**

" *(17)* and ask
the God of our Lord
Jesus Christ, the
glorious Father, to give
you the Spirit, who will

make you wise and reveal God to you, so that you will know him.

(18) I ask that your minds may be opened to see his light, so that you will know what is the hope to which he has called you, how rich are the wonderful blessings he

promises his people,

(19) and how very great is his power at work in us who believe. This power working in us is the same as the mighty strength

(20) which he used when he raised Christ from death and

seated him at his right side in the heavenly world.

(21) Christ rules there above all heavenly rulers, authorities, powers, and lords; he has a title superior to all titles of authority in this world and in the next.

(22) God put all things under Christ's feet and gave him to the church as supreme Lord over all things.

(23) The church is Christ's body, the completion of him who himself completes all things everywhere."

# Colossians 1 : 3 - 6.

" (3) We always give thanks to God, the Father of our Lord Jesus Christ, when we pray for you.

(4) For we have heard of your faith in Christ Jesus and of your

love for all God's people.
(5) When the
true message, the Good
News, first came to you,
you heard about the hope
it offers. So your faith
and love are based on
what you hope for, which
is kept safe for you in
heaven.
(6) The gospel
keeps bringing blessings

and is spreading throughout the world, just as it has among you ever since the day you first heard about the grace of God and came to know it as it really is."

1 Timothy 6 : 17 - 19.

162

" (17) Command those who are rich in the things of this life not to be proud, but to place their hope, not in such an uncertain things as riches, but in God, who generously gives us everything for our enjoyment.

(18) Command them to do good, to be

rich in good works, to be generous and ready to share with others.

(19) In this way they will store up for themselves a treasure which will be a solid foundation for the future. And then they will be able to win the life which is true life."

**6.**

This chapter will be ..... focused on Jeremiah 29 : 11?

180

This book is largely about the very implications of Jeremiah 29 : 11? What it has to say to us in terms of the current situation in the world - at-large with Covid - 19. My belief , is

that this very
verse from
Jeremiah 29 : 11
speaks into the
current situation
we all face with
Covid - 19?
That's if we let it
and and
prepared to hear

what it is saying
to us.

The situation
of the disaster
of the exile and
the resultant
destruction of
Jerusalem is
where the verse
from Jeremiah

comes out of. I would believe that there are many and varied associations between what we are now facing and the times of the exile of the people of the Lord God Almighty. The

nations of the
world - at - large
are being shaken
and stirred in
ways like never
seen in the times
since the year
2,000. I would
believe that
Jeremiah 29 : 11
offers us all much

185

HOPE in the Lord
God Almighty and
a FUTURE in Him.
This goes for the
whole world - at -
large and also
specifically for
the Body of the
Lord Jesus Christ
worldwide?

**186**

There are three major words which come out of Jeremiah 29 : 11; they are the words PLANS, HOPE and a FUTURE. Let us firstly deal with the word Plans? This works on two levels; one the individual level and the other macro level or the whole world - at - large level. I believe that the Lord God Almighty has His

Plans or is it His Will for each individual's life. To a degree, to some this seems rather deterministic on the part of the Lord God Almighty. Yet, in it there is some

security, real
security offered
by it. Therefore,
there is a Plan ,
and your life will
work out
according to the
Plan and the
very Will of the
Lord God
Almighty.

**190**

The main reason why I say there is some sort of security in all of this is because it presumes that there is a Father Lord God Almighty who loves people? All

**191**

of which comes against , by it's very nature , the deterministic view of Plans and life under the very gaze of the Lord God Almighty. The very reality, of the love of the Father changes ...

**192**

everything. As the Lord Jesus Christ was very clear to say in the New Testament Gospels? He makes the point that the Father will not give His children bad things rather He

will love and bless
them. Think about
where He says,
' if you want
bread the Father
will not give you
a stone?' Which
at it's heart
reveals the very
heart and love of
the Father for ...

**194**

people.

Therefore, on one level the Father, the Lord God Almighty works out the Plans for the lives of individual's on the planet. Because it is couched in the ...

very real and lasting love of the Father, the Lord God Almighty. In these times, it is even more and more important to understand this notion and concept; like ......

**196**

never before? As
I sit here writing
this, I am
reminded of the
notion that the
Father, the Lord
God Almighty,
even notes and
acknowledges
when a sparrow
falls and dies. ....

197

How much more will He note and acknowledge when a human being created in His very image , the ' imago deo'; dies .... Something which is worth seeing and even noting

**198**

in these days , we have before us all?

There is also a sense in which He has made Plans for the whole of the World - at - large? Here at this juncture I am thinking about salvation history or redemptive history. This notion is seen in the whole of the Word of God; Genesis to Revelation ... all things working to

the end of
redemption and
salvation and
being around the
very throne of
grace with the
Lord Jesus Christ
seated upon it at
the end of all
things ... the
consummation of ..

201

all things. To make it very simple and plain, the Father, the Son and the Holy Spirit desire that people come home to be with them in heaven and the heavenly city, the New Jerusalem.

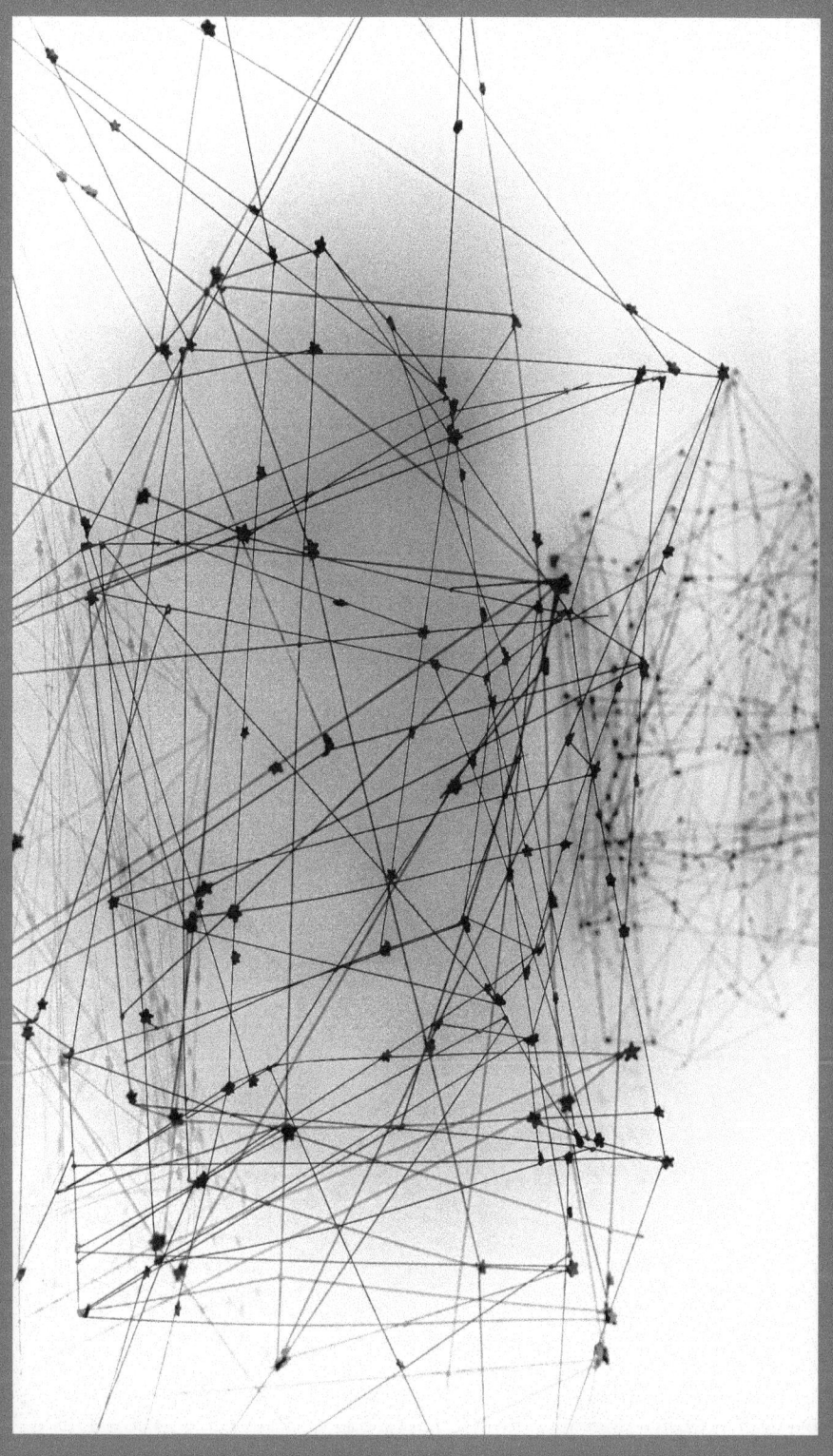

**7.**

This chapter
is a
continuation
of Jeremiah
29 : 11 . Here

the light is
being shone
upon the very
notion and
concept of
HOPE !!!

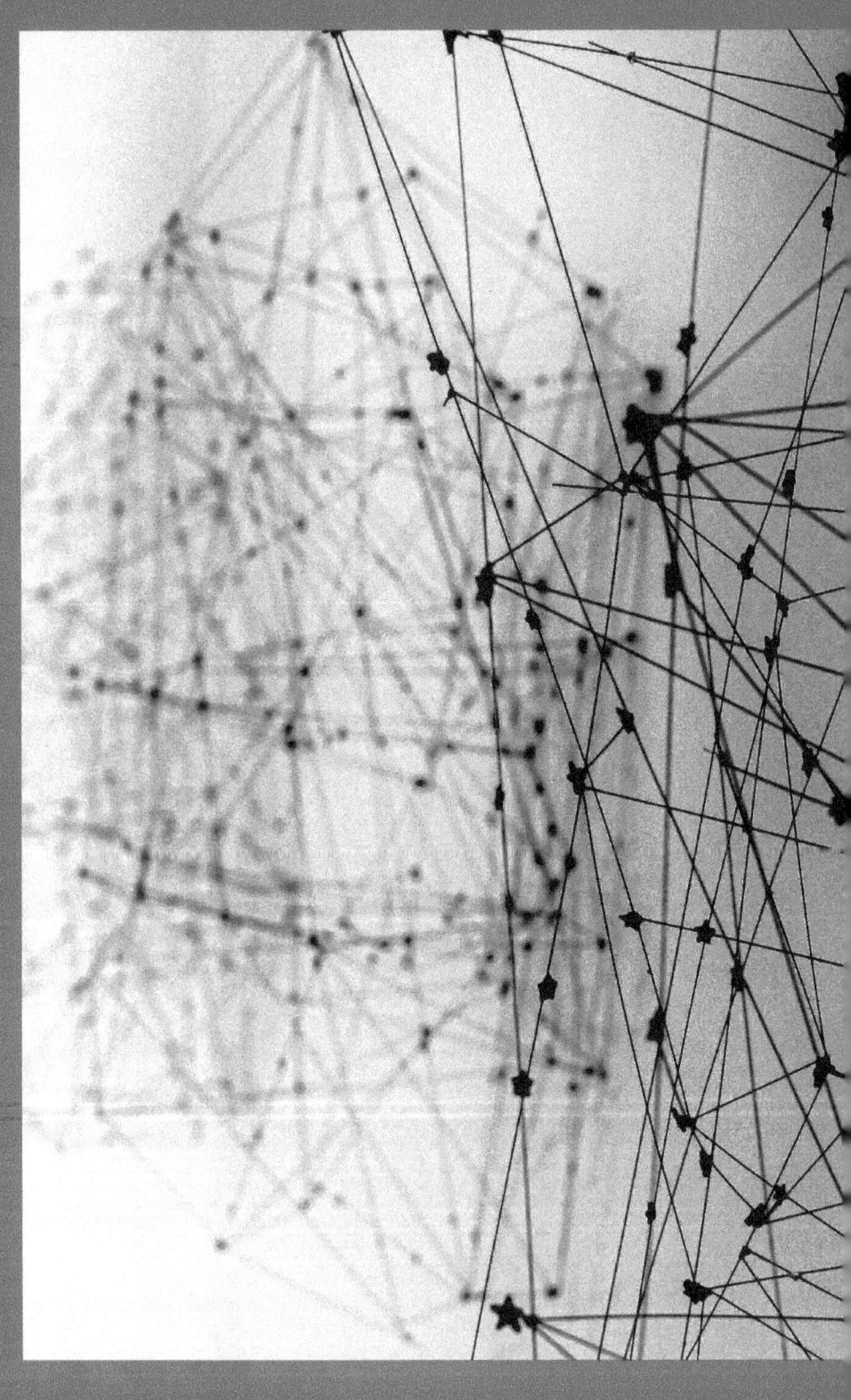

The concept of HOPE is evermore all important in these very days, is it not ...

' Plans to give you hope ....' It is not just that the Lord God Almighty has Plans but also , in

**214**

some ways, more importantly that He has Plans to give us HOPE ! We all in these days need HOPE, as much as they did when they were facing the exilic period in the Old Testament ! But in the end, this to works at both the personal level and the world - at - large level?

At personal level , we all need HOPE for ourselves and our families and even our extended ...

216

families. HOPE is a very ethereal thing, it is a bit like the wind .. it blows about ... comes and goes ... and sometimes can be hard to tie down and even gain for ourselves? In some ways, it all depends what your

**217**

HOPE is grounded
in and even
founded upon.
Our HOPE needs
by it's very
nature to be
founded and
grounded upon
the very real
promises and the
Word of the Lord

**218**

God Almighty ... It
is in both these
things that very
real HOPE can
and will be found
by ourselves and
others ...

To a degree,
without real and
viable HOPE
people perish and

**219**

fade away ... Now more than ever we need to be people who have a very real, grounded and alive HOPE in the Father, the Son and the Holy Spirit .. As they say HOPE does ...

220

not disappoint ?
So personal HOPE
in the Father, the
Son and the Holy
Spirit will not
disappoint ....

Let us now
think about HOPE
in relation to the
world - at - large ?

221

At this very time in the world - at - large we all need HOPE, a very real and lasting and effective HOPE. At times, in the world - at - large , HOPE can be in short supply ?Yet,

**222**

I would believe that this where the Body of the Lord Jesus Christ Worldwide needs to and should step in ... We alone have a real HOPE in the Lord Jesus Christ .. Think Romans 8 : 28 ?

**223**

I do not want to be trite and unfeeling at this very time in the world - at - large  ... But the Body of the Lord Jesus Christ .. needs to step up and offer the very real HOPE

**224**

to the world - at - large in these days and weeks and months ... Never before has there been a time for the Body of the Lord Jesus Christ to step up and offer real and lasting HOPE in

the Lord Jesus
Christ to the very
World - at - large.
That the Father
loved so much that
He sent His own
Son into it to die
upon the very
Cross of Calvary
for all it's failures.

226

In some ways, the offering of real HOPE to the world - at - large comes out of the Body of the Lord Jesus Christ being and becoming ' salt and light' to it?

227

The Father, the Son and the Holy Spirit want to offer the World - at - large HOPE and it starts with the Body of the Lord Jesus Christ offering it to the world - at - large. He has plans to ..

228

give the World - at
- large HOPE ..
and sometimes
that's all it takes?
He gives and
offers the world -
at - large HOPE ,
and the ways and
the means of real
change in these
days !

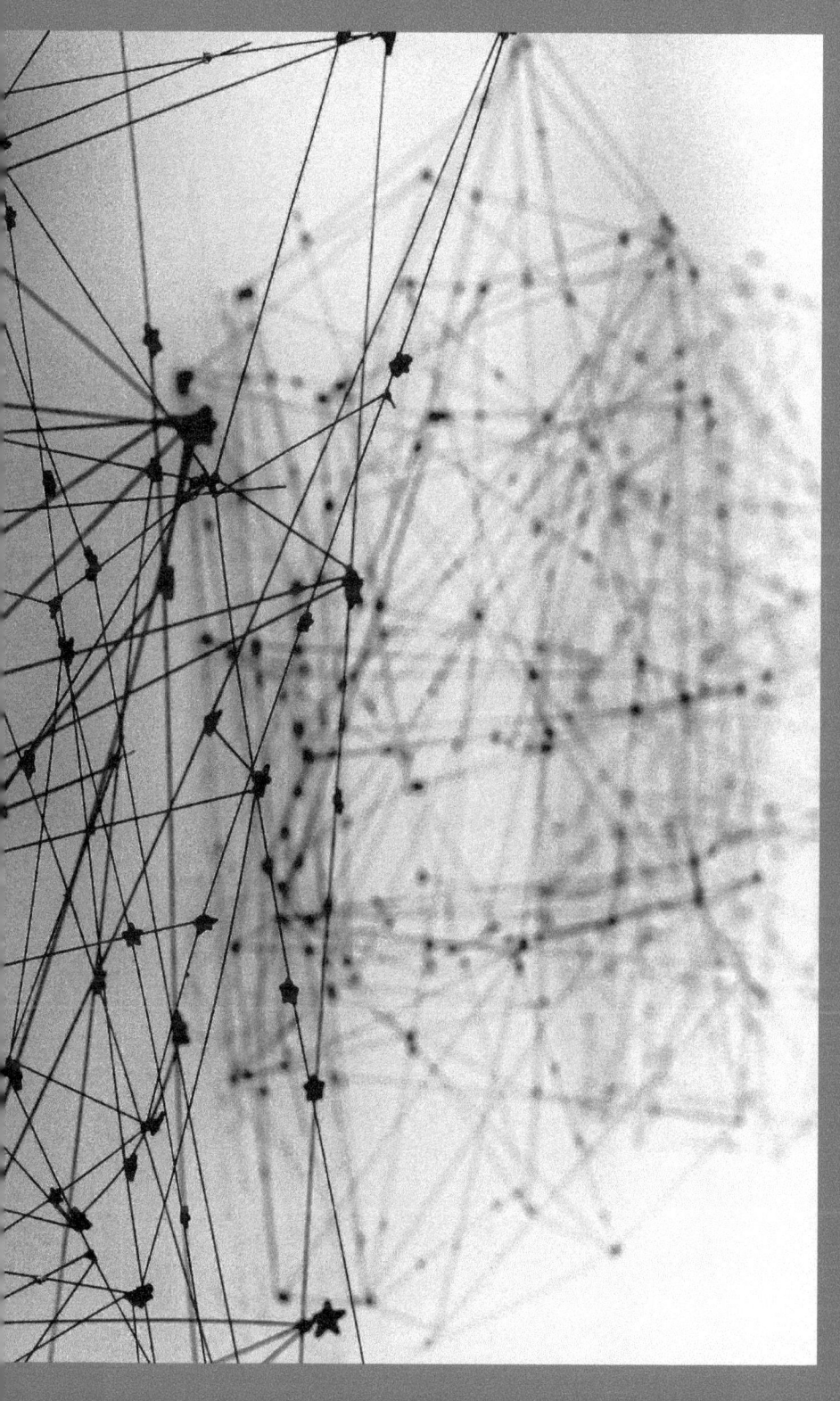

**8.**

This chapter of the book will focus on the words ' a future ' ?

238

We will look at what this looks like in the here and now and beyond as well; beyond Covid - 19?

We have come
to the point of
considering the
words ' a
future'? There is
' a future ' for
those who are
caught up in the

**242**

disaster which is
Covid - 19. I find
this word so
encouraging and
profound at the
same time. There
is both ' a
future' for those
individual's who
are followers of
the Lord Jesus ...

Christ, think the heavenly city, the new Jerusalem and a eternity with the Lord God Almighty. Also, I would believe what is on show through these words is ' a future ' for ..

**244**

the world - at -
large? PLANS ,
HOPE and A
FUTURE all tie in
together , you
need one part of
the equation to
have the rest ...
This is true in
terms of ' a
future ' as well !

I would
believe that the
' a future ' will
be different than
some of us within
the society may
think ... Yet,
there remains a
very real future
in the Lord Jesus

**246**

Christ .. for
those who follow
Him ...and also
for the world -
at - large ...
Think about how
the Lord God
Almighty
' makes the rain
fall on the just
and the unjust?'

247

I would simply believe that the Lord God Almighty, the Father, the Son and the Holy Spirit will have MERCY and there will in fact be ' a future ' for the world - at - large

**248**

as we know it!

All of which is why write a book such as this one. I want to give HOPE FOR A FUTURE to all people based on the very PLANS of the Lord God

Almighty! My prayer, is that, in the very midst of this crisis, you find some time to thank the Lord God Almighty for the mercies in your own life and the life of your immediate and

extended family?
In the end, a lot
of things start
and end with
having a heart
that is grateful ..
and overflows
with gratitude to
the Lord God
Almighty for His
mercies , which..

251

are new every
morning, or so it
is said in the
Word of God !
Related to all this
we all need to
remember and
take on - board
the very reality
that we serve a

252

Lord God Almighty, the Father, the Son and the Holy Spirit who is creating ... and making creations all the time ... and will be for time immemorial !!!

253

# 9.

In this chapter we will be focusing on Proverbs 23 :

264

18 and see what it has to say to us all about the Plans, the Hope and the Future in the Lord God Almighty ?

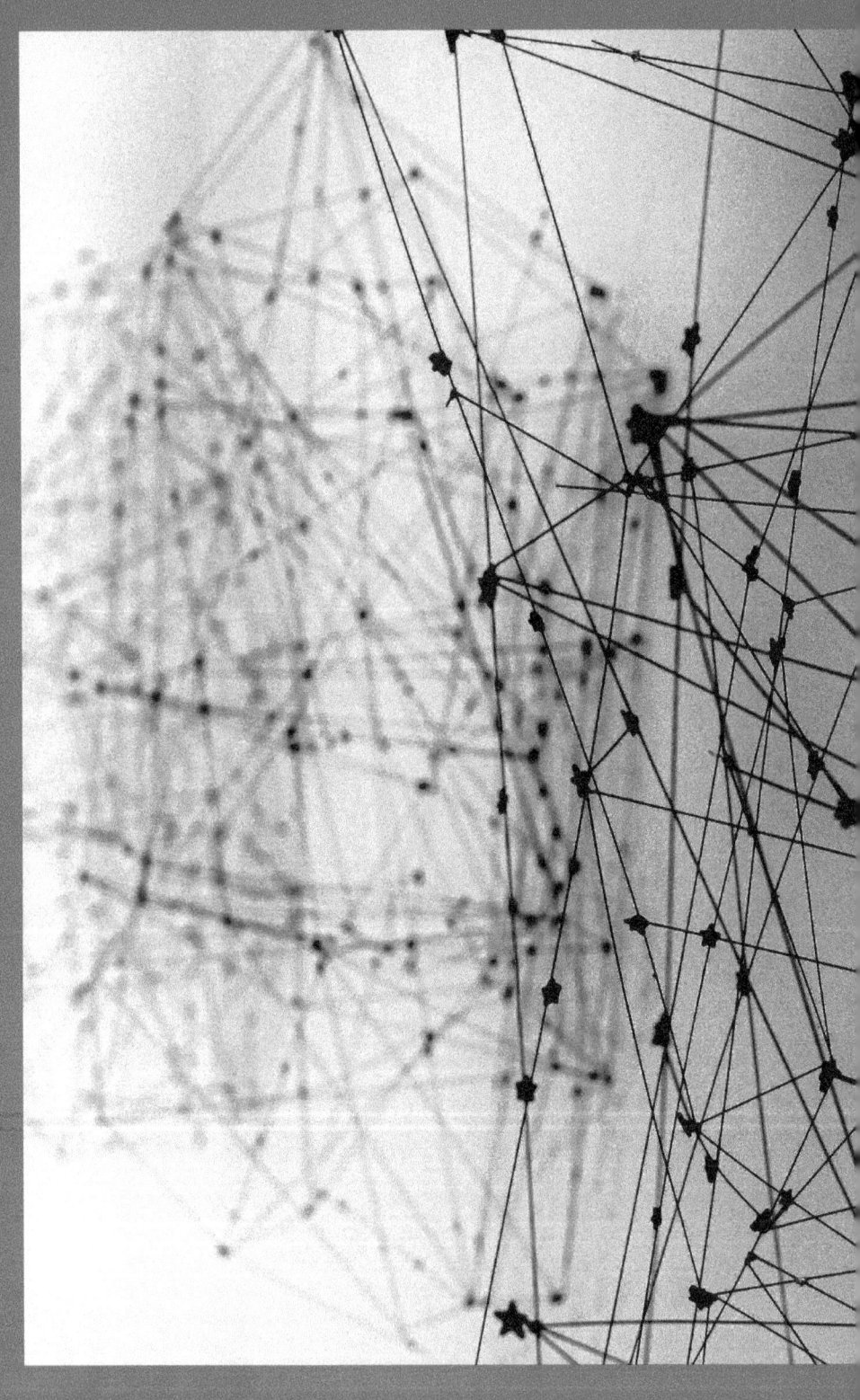

Now we will
spend some time
thinking about
what Proverbs
23 : 18 is saying
to us all? I love
this verse
because it offers

HOPE and A FUTURE in the Lord God Almighty. In some ways, it opens with the after thought of ' Surely there is a future '? In the days of the Proverbs this ...

was a question to ask which came out of wisdom, real Godly Wisdom? It is right and good to always be pondering this very question and to even be asking it out aloud of ...

our selves and others in our world. In some ways, it is this very question which is on the very lips of so many people in the days of Covid - 19? 'Surely there is a future?'

271

The answer that you come up with to this very question individually and corporately is what it is all about in these days that are presently before us. The short ...

answer of this book to this very real question in our days and in our generations is an interesting one? As a Follower of the Lord Jesus Christ I would believe in the affirmative in terms of this question for our days and in our generations. As we have already seen from Jeremiah 29 : 11, we have ' a future' in the Lord God Almighty and this

is something that
while it can be
shaken can never
be taken away
from the abiding
and faithful
follower's of the
Lord Jesus Christ.
So, in the end
' surely there is a
future ?'

I now want
to deal with the
second clause of
the verse from
Provers 23 : 18?
That is, ' and your
hope will not be
cut off.' One could

think big picture
in relation to this
and see that our
hope and our real
hopes for the
future will not be
cut off. It is so
easy in these
times of Covid -
19 for our 'hope
to be cut off?'

In terms of this I am reminded of the words of the Word of God , that HOPE in the Lord God Almighty will not , never disappoint us! In the end, it all depends upon ...

**280**

where your HOPE
lies ... is it in a
better, bigger and
bolder world - at -
large. Or is
rightly I would
believe in the
greater cause and
Kingdom of God
and it coming to
fruition and
becoming full -

**281**

blown in the world - at - large , the very world that the Father loves so much that He sent and gave His own Son, the Lord Jesus Christ to it?

There is HOPE but it may

not be the HOPE some look for or think will happen? In the end, we all need to understand that the world - at - large and all the creation rightly belong to the Lord God Almighty. It

is He who decides
what the HOPE
and the FUTURE
look like for all of
the Creation;
Humanity - at -
large included ....
...Yet our HOPE in
HIM will not be cut
off ?

284

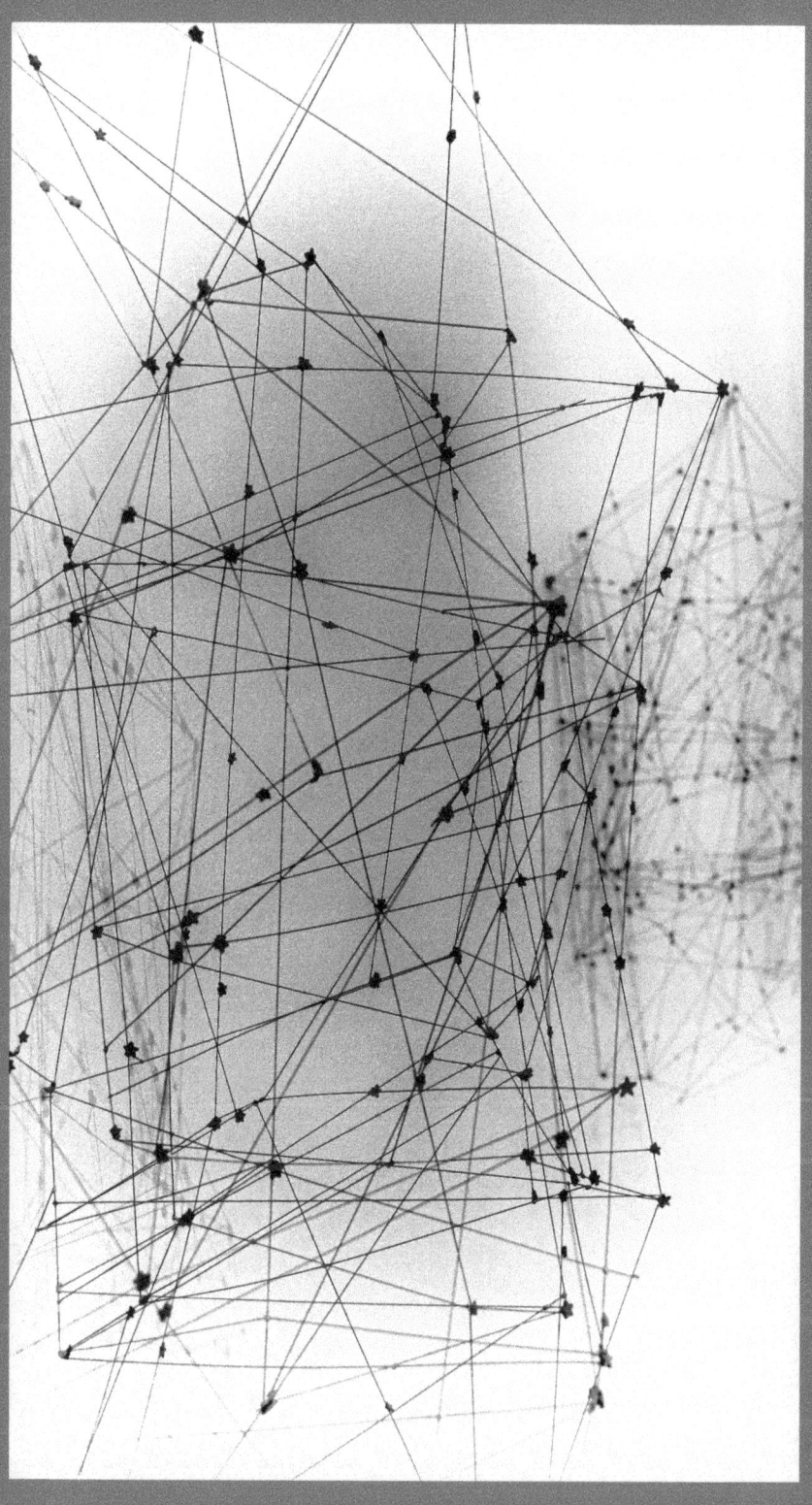

# 10.

In this chapter we will be focusing on Luke 21 : 25 -

28 and what it has to say to us? These verses relate to the current situation in major ways!

Luke 21 : 25 -
28 { ESV }
        " (25) " And
there will be
signs in sun and
moon and stars,
and on the earth

**296**

distress of nations in perplexity because of the roaring of the sea and the waves, (26) people fainting with fear and with foreboding of ...

what is coming
on the world. For
the powers of
the heavens will
be shaken.

(27) And
then they will
see the Son of
Man coming in a
cloud with power
and great glory.

**298**

(28) Now when these things begin to take place, straighten up and raise your heads, because your redemption is drawing near."

To read
these very verses
is rather sobering,
they are profound
and pregnant
with meaning and
implications?
They also relate ..

300

to Jeremiah 29 : 11 in very real ways as well as to the situations that the world - at - large is now facing with Covid - 19. The nations of the world - at - large are certainly in distress and there is a whole lot of fear around ... To see this , all you have to do is to watch the TV news for a minute .. Yet these verses from Luke 21 : 25 - 28 offer some real ..

302

hope , sustained HOPE into the very situations the world-at- large and the nations of it find themselves in it at present with Covid - 19?

Whether or not the Son of God, the Lord Jesus ..

303

Christ's return and second coming is imminent is debatable? In the end, these verses offer real and sustained HOPE, nothing that is happening in the

world - at - large
and it's various
nations surprises
the Lord God
Almighty .. He
had
foreknowledge
that it would
happen ...He has
PLANS, HOPE
and A FUTURE !

**305**

The amazing thing to grapple with , is that, the Word of God does and will speak into our lives and the situations the nations and the world - at - large find themselves in at the present

**306**

time. That is if we let them speak to us all? There is so much fear around at the present moment ... and these verses address this ...they are a great antidote to it ... as they say ' perfect love casts out all fear.' There is in the end, a great HOPE and a great FUTURE to be found in following and believing in the LORD GOD ALMIGHTY, through the very SON OF GOD, the LORD JESUS ...

**308**

CHRIST ... our REDEMPTION is near and getting closer and closer by the day and days ... The LORD JESUS CHRIST WILL RETURN AS HE PROMISED .. IT WILL HAPPEN AND SOONER THAN WE THINK!

**309**

That is not to
be alarmist but in
the end .. He is
on His way and
has been for
quite some time.
There is the very
real HOPE of
glory for those ..

**310**

who follow the
Son of Man, the
very LORD
JESUS CHRIST.
Finally, note
please that the
Lord God
Almighty does
see the distress
and the very
angst of the very

nations of the world - at - large? He is both active and not silent ... now more than ever is the time for His people throughout the known world-at-large to stand up and be the very

**312**

' salt and light '
He always wanted
them to be in this
present age and
times .. Now is not
the times to be
faint - hearted and
even lukewarm...
but rather it is the
time to stand and
believe ...

313

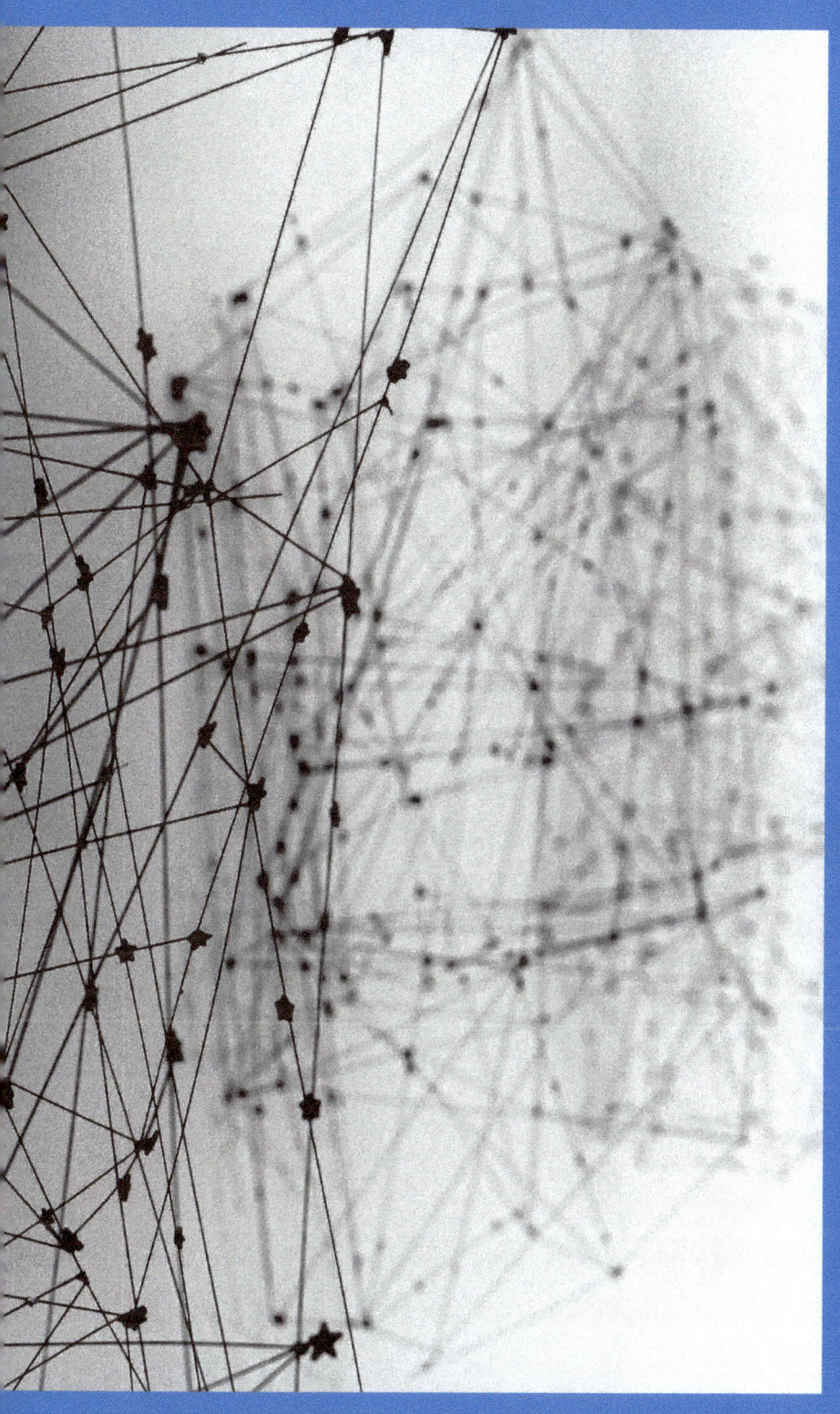

# 11.

As a fitting conclusion to this book we will consider Acts 17 : 30 -

324

31 and what this has to say to us all both in terms of Jeremiah 29 : 11 and the current crisis of Covid - 19?

Acts 17 : 30 - 31.
{ESV}

" (30) The
times of ignorance
God overlooked,
but now he
commands all
people everywhere
to repent,
(31) because

**326**

he has fixed a day on which he will judge the world in righteousness by a man who he has appointed; and of this he has given assurance to all by raising him from the dead. "

327

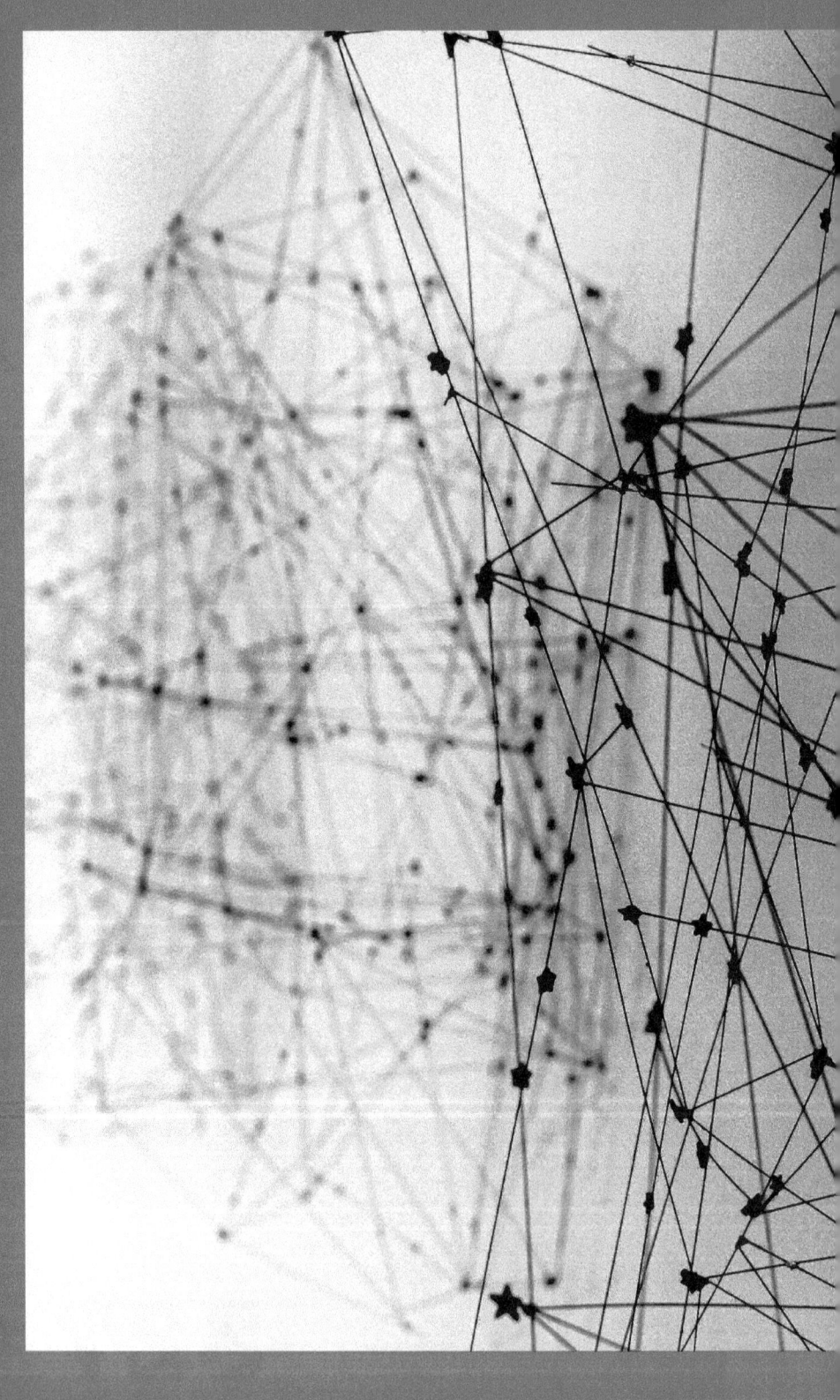

These words
from the hand of
the Apostle Paul,
need to resound
even the more-so
with us in our
days and in our
generations ? One

**334**

cannot however
much one tries to,
get away from the
very command of
the Lord God
Almighty for
people
everywhere to
REPENT ! Not
only to REPENT
but to RETURN to

HOME to HIM, the Father, the Son of God, the Lord Jesus Christ and the Holy Spirit. There is much we in the Western Civilization need to be repenting of and the very ....

**336**

command of the
Lord God Almighty
is to do it NOW!
But in so many
ways, I see this as
the prodigal sons
and daughters of
the Lord God
Almighty just
being asked to
RETURN HOME to

337

HIM?

In the end, the day of salvation is NOW and NOT LATER! One cannot water down the very clear command of the Lord God Almighty through the Apostle Paul!

**338**

The clarion call of the Lord God Almighty is for as it has always been for people everywhere to REPENT and RETURN HOME TO HIM, as the waiting and the expectant FATHER!

339

There is a clear, very clear connection between Jeremiah 29 : 11 and these particular verses? In terms of the PLANS, the HOPE and the FUTURE in the Lord God Almighty they are

**340**

all caught up
with the very
real call to
REPENT !!!! Now
is the very time
to be REPENTING
before the Lord
God Almighty,
seize the day ..
now is the time
of salvation !!!

341

As to why
REPENT ... and
now ; it is because
the day of
judgment by the
Son of God, the
Lord Jesus Christ
is coming and is a
reality ! This is ...

342

the very real
import of verse
31 .... There is
coming a day of
judgment .. before
the Son of Man,
the Lord Jesus
Christ ... All of
which is why
there is a real
need to REPENT !

**343**

The assurance and the guarantee of all this being the simple and yet profound TRUTH is the resurrection from the DEAD of the very Son of God, the Lord Jesus Christ. If ...

344

one sees that as
not being truth,
then one does not
have to listen ...
But the clarion
call of Paul and
myself is for all
people everywhere
to REPENT before
the Lord God
Almighty !

345

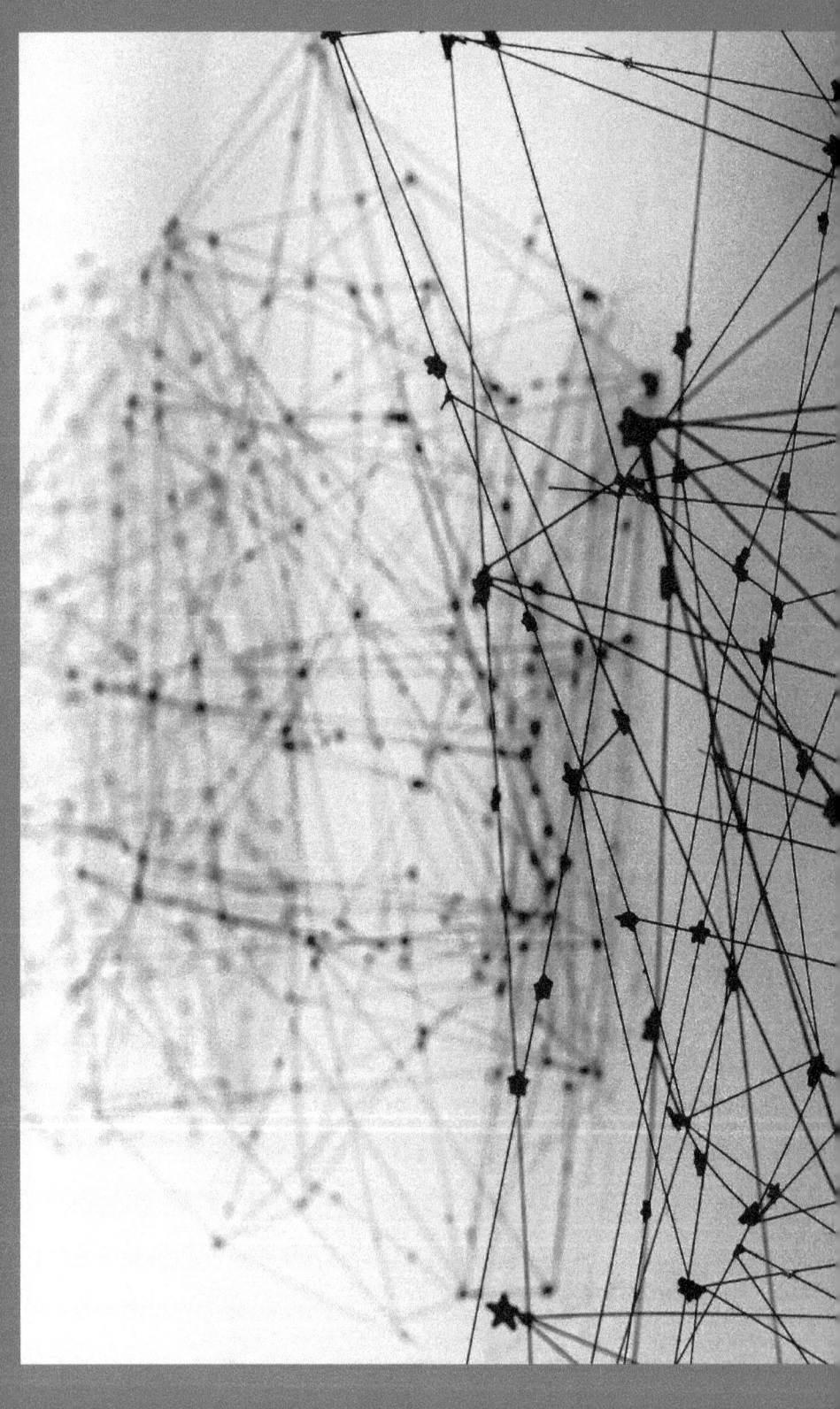

# 12.

## EPILOGUE :

To sum up or
even dare I say
conclude this very
book, let us think
about Jeremiah

29 : 11 and the words ; PLANS, the HOPE and a FUTURE. Let these very words from the Word of God ring and resound in your minds and your hearts! The Lord God Almighty who did

**363**

say them to
Jeremiah the
Prophet is the
same Lord God
Almighty, the
Father, the Son of
God, the Lord
Jesus Christ and
the Holy Spirit
today as He was

**364**

in the days of
Jeremiah.
   PLANS
   HOPE
   A FUTURE !

These three
things are to be
found in and
through a abiding
relationship with

**365**

the Father, the
Son of God, the
Lord Jesus Christ
and the Holy
Spirit....May you
come to accept
just how much
the Father ... the
Lord God
Almighty desires
all people to .....

**366**

come HOME to HIM!

So, please come HOME to HIM .... Time is of the essence , in these days of Covid - 19 and it's effects throughout the world - at - large!

367

The World - at -
Large that the
Father loved so
much that He
sent His One and
Only Son, the
Lord Jesus
Christ into it to
die a cruel and
nasty death upon

368

the Cross of
Calvary to pay
for the
wrongdoing of
the it past,
present and
future.
Remember :
PLANS...
HOPE....
A FUTURE !!!

369

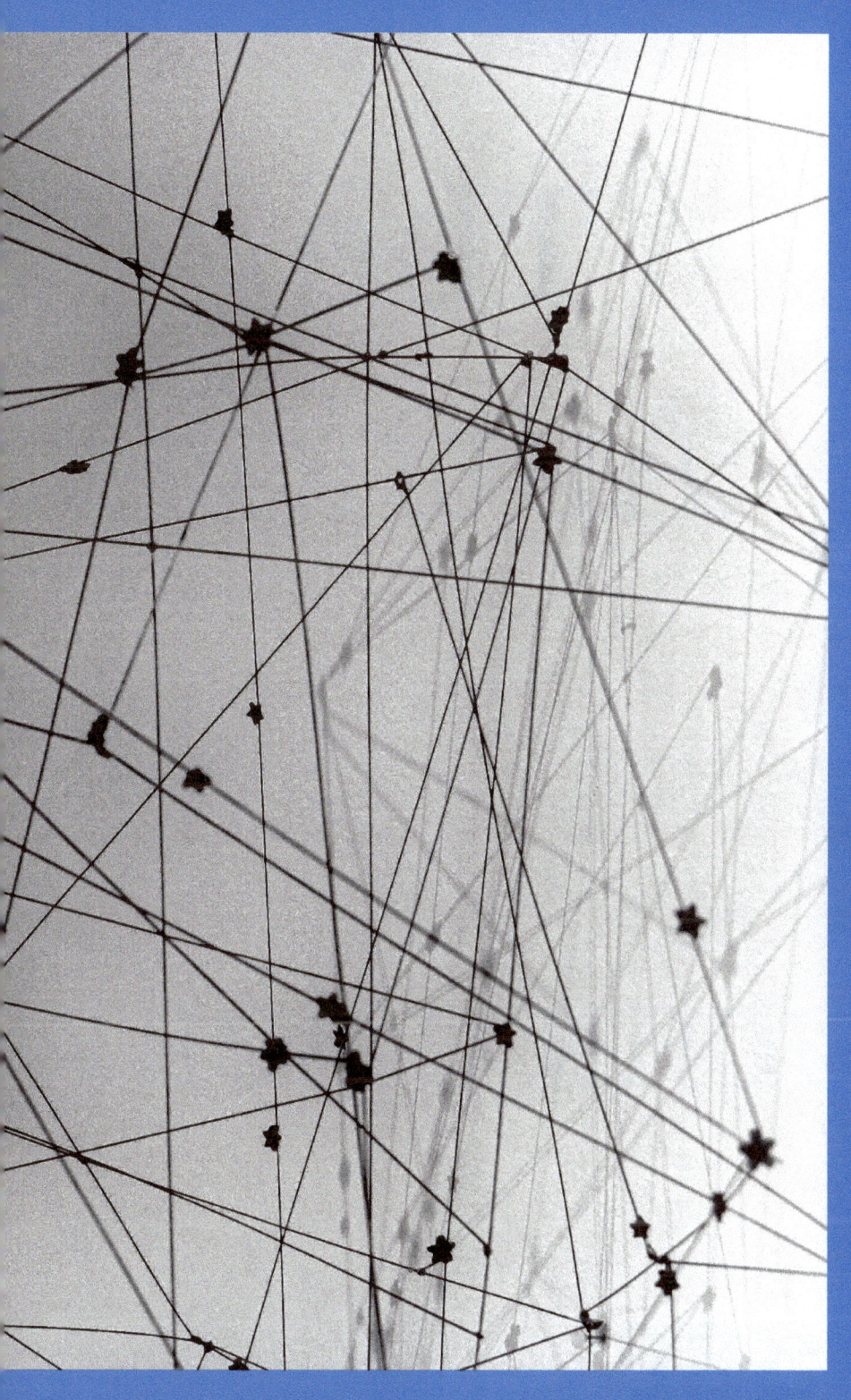

# The Author:

## JOHN C BURT

**386**

# JOHN STILL GOES TO A CHURCH .. A FOLLOWER OF THE LORD JESUS CHRIST FOR

**388**

FOR FORTY
THREE
YEARS ..
IT IS AN
ABIDING
FRIENDSHIP
WITH THE
LORD JESUS!

**389**

JOHN LOVES FOOTBALL, CRICKET AND ALL AND ANY FORMS OF SPORT ...

390

JOHN LOVES COFFEE, HOT AND STRONG AS STRONG ! AS WELL AS PIZZA, CHICKEN AND JELLYFISH; SERVED COLD!

391

# AMEN and AMEN...

392

# SHALOM:

DEAR LORD JESUS; THANK YOU AND HELP ME TO APPLY YOUR PLANS, HOPE AND THE FUTURE TO MY LIFE !

AMEN ...

393

394

395

400

402

403